What Can I Learn?

art and poetry

by

Mary Lee George

P.O. 14593
Minneapolis, MN 55414

First edition. First printing. April 9983 (1983)

Typesetting and quackery by duck type, Minneapolis, Minnesota
Layout and design by Mary Lee George
Printed by the Iowa City Women's Press, Iowa City, Iowa

ISBN 0-9610930-0-5

I learn from everything in my life: the earth, people, plants, rocks, animals, the elements, the heavens. This book was written to share some of what I've learned from my own experience and by listening to other women. From my mother, Eloise George, I received the money to publish this book and a valuable model for writing things down. Through her letters, she shares her life with me in a unique way. I treasure them and her influence on me. She taught me to be a writer. From my offspring, Mindy, Georgia, Adam and Dan, I have learned how to live and to forgive myself. From my friends Rachel, Terri, Shirley and Kathy I receive encouragement and feminist critique that helps me be who I am, to act on what is deepest and highest in me and to put some of that down on paper. This book is about and for all the women in my life who share their life with me so that I continue to learn and grow.

Mary Lee George

Solstice 9982   a.d.a.*

*a.d.a.—after the development of agriculture

To Pamela,

May your exploration of life bring you home to yourself.

Blessed Be

Antiga (Mary Lee)

12-8-85

I've known Mary Lee for eight and a half years. We met at a women's writing class. That class grew into a writing group named Atlantis which still meets regularly. Atlantis members share our writing and editing skills with each other. We also share our lives. Mary Lee says that **What Can I Learn?** was birthed in Atlantis. I am pleased to have been one of the midwives.

As an introduction to Mary Lee and her book, I'd like to share with you some of the things that I've learned from her.

I've learned that change, while frightening, can be embraced; and that the act of accepting change brings comfort.

I've learned that sharing my feelings with others and with myself expresses, as well as facilitates, growth.

I've learned to see my own wisdom as valuable.

I've watched Mary Lee "promptly admit it" when wrong and thoroughly enjoy it when right, and have learned that it is possible to like oneself.

I'm learning to allow others to love me unconditionally and therefore, that it is possible to love myself.

I've watched Mary Lee singing and learned what the words "enjoy yourself" really mean.

I've watched Mary Lee become a leader in the women's spirituality movement and learned what the word courage means.

I watch Mary Lee embrace her crone years and learn that it is possible to face my fear of aging and death.

I've learned that in a world where there are few role models for women, we can be examples for each other.

Rachel Walker
February 1983

The Flow

III What can I learn from the circle?

IV What can I learn from the elements?

VI What can I learn from my friends?

VII What can I learn from learning?

1

What can I learn beginning?

What can I learn beginning?

**I am born into the light
It hurts my eyes at first
Beginning to breathe
Beginning to love
Beginning to listen
Beginning to write
Beginning to BE
Who I am
Wanting to bleed
Wanting to birth
Wanting to blossom
Knowing that I can**

2

Creativity
Pulsates
Pauses
Tenses
Pauses
Pushes
Pauses
Creativity
Births itself
Creativity
Flows   Connects
Flowers   Centers
Flows   Curls
Flames   Centers
Flows   Coils
Floats   Centers
Creativity Circles
Centers

II

What can I learn from nature?

What can I learn from the birds?

**You fly high
And see us
    as smaller than yourselves
      perhaps
    unable to lift ourselves
    off the ground and soar**

**You light on an earth-bound tree
Your song floats clear and free**

**I can learn to let my song soar
    like your flight**

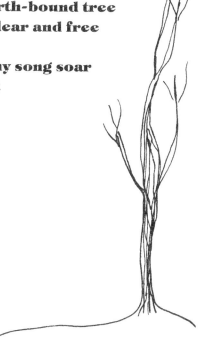

What can I learn from the bee?

The bee flies
    to the
    luscious
    purple
    thistle blossom
She lands in the soft flower
    entirely
    avoiding
    the thistle spikes

spider

You leap into space
spinning a connection
to your center
as you go.

With
a strong
seemingly fragile
thread
You weave a web
delicate and
beautiful
to sustain
yourself.

I can learn
faith to leap
with the knowledge that
I am spinning
a connection
back to
my center.

What can I learn from the snake?

Using all of your body, you glide
    over the ground
A sensuous creature
People fear you
    strength
      and
    sensitivity

Like you, I can use my whole body
    to move forward
    unable
    to go back
    where I've been
    without forward motion

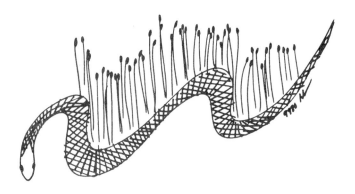

algae

The lake edge is thick with 13
     shades of green
You are a water color on the water
Floating by in serpent/dragon
     shapes

dragonfly

You fly soundlessly
    lighting gently
    silence the buzzing mosquito
    quietly   carefully   deliberately
Taking it into your iridescent body

What can I learn from the ant?

You, the strong sister,
Carry a wounded sister
 Struggling with the weight of two
        You rest
          then
        Pick up your burden
          again
        Rest again and
        Go on once more
Finally you leave her immobile
    on the rock
Do you go for help?
Or do you leave knowing that
    she is beyond help?

What can I learn from the cat?

Upon waking
You stretch each muscle
    slowly
    carefully
Before moving into the activity
    of the day

What can I learn from Isis?

Green eyes
Black fur
Black whiskers
You know a kindred spirit
When you see her

You join me in the hammock
Lie on my lap
Let my hands smooth
    your silky fur

Watchful and sleek
You look at me
You look away
Allowing me to see your profile

Dusk darkens
Your fur blends with the night
You are Bast, Artemis and Isis
You share your essence with me

lynx

Your soft grey beauty
Is tipped with black
    ear edges and tail
Your large paws carry you
    silently over snow
        over rocks
        over grass
To hunt for food or
To where you can soak up
    the midday sun

beaver

You are called "busy" by people who
    watch you
You cut down a 3 inch aspen trunk
    in a minute
The ducks scatter as it hits the water
You drag the aspen over the dam and
    into winter storage for food
After being busy all fall
You slow your pace to near
    stay-still in winter

dolphin

Your grey and white skin turns
    pink on your belly
It looks so smooth that I want
    to touch it
You turn on your side to see us
    an eye on either side of your head
What must it be like to receive
    a different image in each eye
And how do you integrate
    the two?

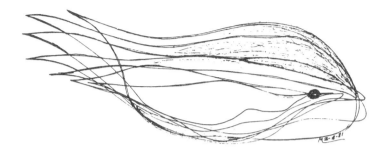

whale

Your song is complex and eerie
Changing from year to year
You travel great distances to mate
    and to eat
The ocean of a whole hemisphere is
    your home
Patterns on your tail tell people
    who you are
You make a spiral bubble net
    eating plankton
  as you rise
You survive
    in tune with your
      intelligence
    one with the elements
      water and air

What can I learn watching the moon set?

Tonight, you are half full
  You hide on the other side
    of a cloud
  You come forth blurry
    thin clouds around you
      then clear as the clouds disappear
  Deep yellow as you approach
    the horizon
  I see you behind the trees
    above the water
      as you descend to play
        with your
          sister Earth

The sun has set
   in the valley below
It still shines high atop the hill
   where I stand
   shrouded in purple
   in a grove of trees
   ground covered with soft green grass
   listening to the birds' cacophony
   as they settle on their roost to sleep,
   watching the clouds
   reflected in the lake
   waiting for
The sun to set
   behind Minnesota farmland
   coloring the sky rosy

The image of a woman appears
   in a fallen tree trunk
I am alone
And wish it so

What can I learn from the Equinox?

Day and night are equal
Balance is achieved.
Equality lasts
    such a short while
I want it for longer
Scrolls wind and unwind
Nothing stays as it is

What can I learn from the seasons?

Light returns and darkness recedes
Dark returns and light recedes
Day and night take their turns
The sun burns hot
The night comes cold
The seasons melt into one another
What has been will come again
What will be has already begun

What can I learn valuing winter in my life?

I can learn to snuggle in
to slumber
I can explore my inside
I can accept my sickness
the inevitability of my death
I can see my underside
in darkness

at springtime

**I can learn that life and warmth
return
after ice
after cold
after dark
Light returns and
Flowers bloom**

summer

Light is at its height
Outdoors begs to be explored
    canoeing
    hiking
    swimming
The creatures of the world and I
    frolic
    play and
    work to stay alive

fall

Cold comes quietly
Darkness deepens
Harvest in the air
We store up for winter
    amid the brilliant
    turning colors

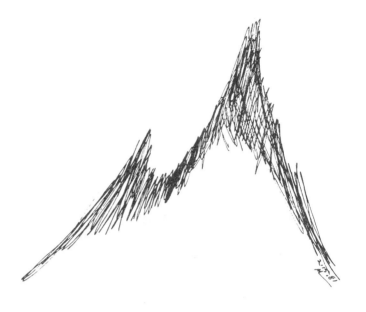

mountain

I climb to your top
    and see for a great distance
I enter your caverns
    and feel the darkest dark
You are both light and dark
        far and near
You comfort me
You cradle me
Mountain where I was born

morning glory

You open up
in the morning
taking the sun
into your
pentacle center
soft
brilliant blue
surrounded
by your sisters
You close
when the sun
leaves you

You know
when to open
and when to close

What can I learn from the square?

**A shape virtually never
appearing naturally
A shape built by men
to contain their
possessions**

III

What can I learn from the circle?

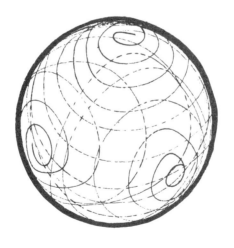

What can I learn from the circle?

Your edges are smooth and curved
Each point on your circumference
  is of equal value
You have no beginning nor end
You are the basic form found in nature
You are the nurturing breast
  the seeing eye
You are open at your center

spiral

You are a circle
cycling
In a different dimension
Conch shell
Inner ear
Galaxy

stars

Small-seeming, brilliant circles of light
Your radiance seems to be pointed
Your patterns in the sky are
so striking
That people tell tales about you

sun

Circle of light and energy
Radiating life giving
   life sustaining heat
You rise each morning
Though sometimes covered by clouds
Your light shines through
You are always there

moon

Circle of reflected light
Ever changing
You show us
a different phase
of your face
every night
From crescent
to quarter
to full
to quarter
to crescent
to DARK
You
always cycle 'round again

What can I learn from the crystal ball?

Seeing through you
You MAGNIFY
the small stone goddess
close to your crystal sphere
You turn Her upside down
as I move Her away from you

Between—
At the turning point
You curve the image around
your edge
Until it meets itself again
Your magic:
Trans-
forming
vision
so that
I can
see
what a
curved
world
would
be like

rainbow

You dance in the prism
You circle round the crystal ball
You arch across the sky
     all possibilities of color
The Goddess glows in you

IV

What can I learn from the elements?

What can I learn from the fire?

**You leap to Sister Air
She sustains you as
You warm her**

red \ orange   red \ yellow   orange \ yellow

Red   Orange   Yellow

Transforming

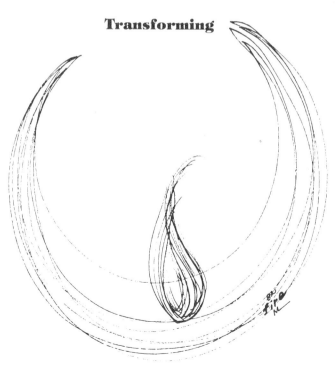

air

You are felt and not seen
You are wild—whistling through the trees
     cooling my cheek
Sometimes you are so still that
You are neither felt nor heard nor seen
Our breath depends on you

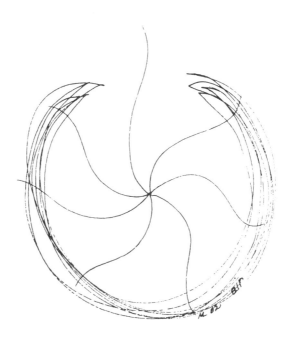

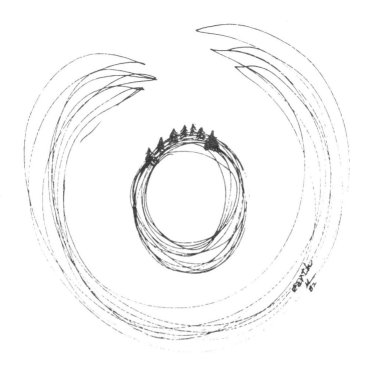

earth

You bring water to your surface
Harbor fire in your depths
Nourish creatures and plants
 giving of yourself
 as you are needed
 Our life depends on you

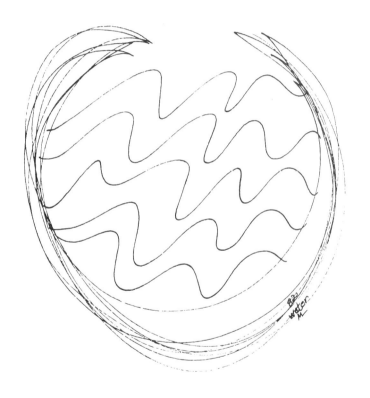

water

**You spring from Mother Earth
You flow on
     filling up the pits
     in your way
You make lovely music
     as you lap the shoreline**

rain

**Sometimes you come when
I don't want you
Sometimes you fail to fall when
you're needed
Sometimes your force destroys
hard gardening work
When you come with the sun
You create a color miracle**

snow

You make beautiful patterns
    on the skylight windows
    as you fall
    forests of white evergreens
              growing
We feel cozy inside watching you float
    outside
You are soft and gentle and white
You melt into the dark stream
              vanishing
You cover trees, people and houses
    alike

rocks

Your size varies from tiny grains of sand
    to huge prehistoric boulders
Your color varies from black-blue to grey
    to white to brown to red to gold
Your shape varies from sharp and straight
    to round and smooth and curved
The gentle water wears you down
Until you crack

What can I learn from the sand?

I can learn who's been here:
People prints
    craters and valleys in your landscape
    small dunes or waves
    atop the larger dune
Snake imprint, curled full circle
    around a dune grass center
Bird prints—three toed tracks
    indenting you
Indiscriminate tracks
    neither clearly
    bird nor animal
        Whose?

Within the within
    is fire
Within the within is
    fire reflected on water
    fire dancing in air
    fire charring the earth
Within the within is
    fire burning me up
    fire charging me into
      new forms
      a new face
    fire charring me
      connecting me to
      deeper awareness
      higher spirit

V

What can I learn living?

What can I learn from my life?

I married at 23
    divorced at 45
    4 children in 6 years
    13 volumes of journal
        my pain indexed
        between the covers

At 47—a spiritual growing
    beginning to be myself
    strong inside and sparing of words
    singing dancing writing
    energy vibrating inside me
    sun shining on top of me
    life flowing with me
    love going from me

I am the tide
I am the moon
I pull myself toward womanhood

Such a warm day
It could be June
I spiral back to
Many Junes ago
The warmth, the tenderness
The feeling, the caring
The loving excitement
Birthing daughters
  Most
  Intimate
  Connection
Creating new life

Honor Harmony Esteem
Needed to grow as daughters grew

   Instead
Sensuous June came round and round
And sensitive daughters found
   Accord
Shattered into tiny splinters
  Broken heart
  Broken dream
  Battered love

What can I learn letting go?

Letting go of my will
Claiming my soul and body
Connecting body and soul
BE-
coming whole

What can I learn doing Tai Chi?

I find my feminine roots—
    going into the earth
I deepen my awareness—
    exploring the depths
I learn to let go
    flowing with the ki
I learn to move
    from my center
I learn to live
    from the inside out
I learn to trust life instead of
    trying to control it

What can I learn from I Ching?

I can learn that
    what is not sought
    in the right way
    in the right place
    is not found
I can learn to be responsible
    for my own actions
I can learn to create
    affirming attitudes
    within myself
        with
      NO BLAME
    toward myself
      or others

"I am forgiving myself
   for being late"
   I tell you

"I like to see you forgive yourself"
   you reply
"but will you change as well?"

I can learn that self-forgiveness
   is necessary but not
     sufficient

simplifying my life

I can learn that I need
     far fewer things
     than I supposed
     to thrive on
I can learn to enjoy
     the here and now
I can agree to do only those things
     that my time and energy
     will comfortably allow

To Matt
What can I learn from your life?

You chose to be with us a short time
You chose to teach us valuable lessons
about love
about courage
about sadness
about grief—
How to use grief to grow on

grieving

I can learn to
    feel the pain
    give up the guilt
I can become
    a different me
Learning
    as I survive
    to be alive

What can I learn from depression?

I can learn to rest
I can learn to take my time
I can learn to let the rest of the world
  go by

What can I learn living alone?

Loneliness often
    aches inside me
Yet it's the price I pay
    for being who I am
Living alone brings me
    more time that's my own to use
    no distractions when I want to work
    no housework when I want to write
    quiet when I need it
    music when I want it
Loneliness is becoming a friend
She still aches inside me
And is a price that's worth the
        pain

growing older

I can learn that
 I do learn
 from living
I learn from the pain
 that opens me
 to joy
I learn that
 my life
 repeats itself
 AND
 that I can change
 old patterns
My wisdom waxes
 as I grow old
I'm going to be a crone

Fear of death is fear of the unknown
Fear of death is really fear of life

Initiation   Transition   Acceptance
            Transcendence
The unknown whirls me around
    in darkness
veined with rivers of light
I float above the forest on the
    edge of the lake
Separation from old patterns
    old habits
Going through the tunnel to the light

Dark lady
    with sparkles around your eyes
        all colors
    emerging out of deeper darkness
    merging into darkness
Fear of death is really fear of life

dreaming

I can visit the places
    I want to visit
I can see the friends
    I want to see
I can do the things
    I want to do
    while dreaming

I can learn to protect myself
    in my dream
Then in my life

Each of us is ordinary
in some way
and
Each of us is extraordinary
special
different
at some time

We need to be ordinary
to fit in
We need to be extraordinary
to stand out

Fitting in/Standing out
Exactly   when   I   need to
Fitting In   Standing Out

What can I learn from the mirror?

Your round face
Circled by golden wood
Shines my face
    back to me
    when I look at you
Brown hair
Winged with silver

Inner beauty glows
    within
Your golden frame

writing

I can learn to condense
I can learn to expand
I can learn to express
I can learn what I feel
I can learn to flow freely
I can learn to revise
I can learn that I'm wise

travelling

**I can learn that there are
other ways of speaking
other ways of thinking
other ways of living**

Do they find me strange?

walking

I can feel the rhythm
   of my body
I can see where I am
   as I walk
I can feel the breeze, the sun
   on my back
I can learn that my body
   will take me
   where I want to go

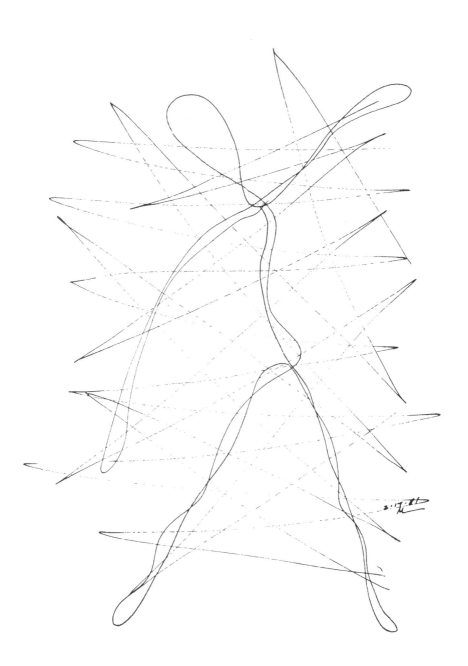

singing

**I can learn to breathe deeply
I can learn to fulfill and nurture
myself
with the fullness
of my voice
I can learn to let my voice out
the open pipe
that my throat is
FREE
I can learn not to stop my voice
by catching it in my throat**

Singing as I swing
   in my childhood swing
Swinging is motion
   Freedom to flow
   Freedom to feel
     air flowing round me
   Freedom to feel that
   I can reach the clouds
     and float away
     over the Blue Ridge
       mountains

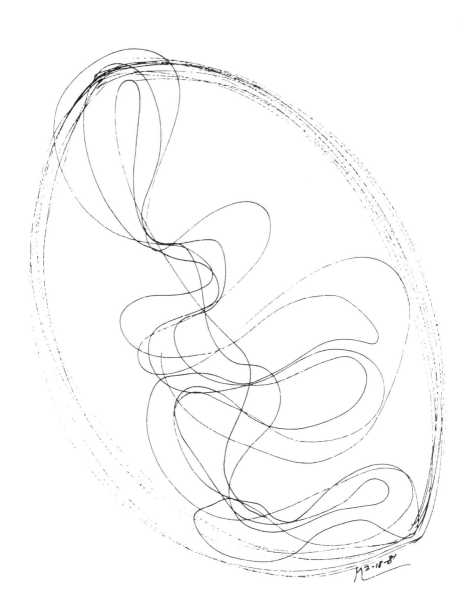

swimming

I feel the water
    get cooler
    as I plunge deeper
Floating, I see the sky above
    cloud fingers reach
    from the horizon
    stretching heaven
    to its limit
Underwater vibrations
    excite me

I can learn to love
Being in another element

What can I learn from doing the laundry?

I notice what disdain we have
for earthly tasks:
cooking sweating and gardening
All stains must be washed away

We sweat and
cook and
dig in the dirt
and have to appear as though
We didn't

I look at my body
    through the water
    while bathing
I discover that
    my navel,
    pushed out after
    carrying four children
Forms the shape of a spiral

The metaphor of female growth

What can I learn from my menstrual blood?

I can feel
    the pull of the moon
        inside me
I can see my life
    cycle round and round again
    joy sadness joy
I can learn
    what it feels like
    to be a woman
I birth life
    with my blood

mothering

**I can learn that, at times,
another's needs
must come before mine.
I learn joy from touching
I feel safety
in caring.
I can teach independence.
I can learn to mother myself too**

**I can learn to accept myself
when my offspring displease me
I can learn that my value
is independent
of what they do**

daughtering

I can learn that what was
        right for your life
        may not be right
            for mine
I can learn to decide for myself
I can learn to accept
        what of you
        is repeated in me
        and not reject it all
            simply
        because it's yours
I can honor your life
        by the way
I live mine

being honest

I can learn
    that honesty
    is not really valued
    nor expected

I can learn
    that the most useful
    and most difficult
    sort of honesty
    to gain
    is self honesty

Pushing my own self honesty
    further and further
I know how essential it is
    for my own growing
    for my own well being

I can learn how scared I am
    to be honest

making choices

I can learn what I value doing
I can learn who I wish
     to spend time with

I can suppose that if she chooses
     to spend time with me
     she values being with me
I can enjoy it when her choice fits
     my wishes
I can love the time we have together
And never ask her to be exclusively
     with me
By my choices, I can cherish
     her choices

I can learn to choose wisely

making mobiles

I can learn what a tiny bit of weight
      changes the balance
I can feel the balance in my hand
      as I add a snowflake, a pine cone
        or a flower
I can enjoy the beauty of your movement
        your flow
      in the slightest current of air
        as I hang you up
      for others to see

Touching is different than talking
I find it hard to explain
I need to touch you to tell you

A different sense
A different feel
Talking touches my mind
Touching talks to my body

Your touch meets a deep need
    primal, almost
Your talk soothes my surface
    satisfying in one way and
      leaves me longing for your touch

Touching is something special
I want it to be everyday

What can I learn being intimate?

I learn that intimacy
Appears
in many forms:
talking
touching
singing
and
most intimate of all
silence

9-20-82

When I love myself first
It doesn't feel like
I'm giving it away when
    I love you
It feels like widening
The circle of my love
    to include
    you
Then love goes
    to and fro
in the shape of infinity
When I let it in
    love
grows as it flows

VI

What can I learn from my friends?

What can I learn from my friends?

The close friends
The valuable friends
    reflect myself back to me
       all my phases
        seeing
       my bare being
        through
      my lovely, angry or aging
        face

What can I learn sistering?

I can learn to trust
I can learn to respect
I can learn that we don't have to compete
     we can help each other
Singing   Centering
   Writing   Walking
     Talking   Painting
        Listening
I share my sistersoul

Rachel

I learn so much
I hardly know where to begin

I begin to count on your love
    and love myself more truly
I begin to trust our trust
    and rely on myself more fully
I count on your honesty
    and see myself more clearly

Clearly, fully and truly
You are my dear and caring friend

What I learn from you never ends

Terri

I can learn that
      however scared I am
It's OK to tell you I'm angry

While separate from a family
      that I love
I can create another family
With you in the center

Maggie

Our running song is good for walking too
You run
I walk
You ride your bicycle to California
I fly to California
You are both slower and faster than I am
    AND
We can walk together

Kathy

You illustrate feminism
    from the inside out
Inviting me to explore intricacies inside:
    other views/different concerns
Clearly rooted in a feminist
    core that's always there
    to amaze me
Our ideas flow and change
    as we toss them
    back and forth

    With you
I can plan peace
In a world
    weary with
    warped by
                war axioms

What do I learn from Nancy?

I learn to read music
I learn to feel the tempo, the tone
   in my body
I learn to sing on pitch
I learn to sing notes from memory
   pull an "A" out of the air
I learn what color my voice is
I learn to sing through
   the dolphin spout in my nose
I learn excellence
   combined with caring

Julia

I can learn that
    being a competent businesswoman
    and a fine artist
    are compatible activities
I can learn to surround myself
    with beauty and simplicity
I can learn to paint my pictures large

Mona

I can learn to listen to
    your life
I can learn to share my life,
    my art
    my feminism
    with you
I can learn that art is life
    is spirituality
That spirituality is
    the art of living

Rainbow woman

**Love and passion
    light up your face
Letting your inner beauty
    come out
        to delight me
        to invite me
        to weave into mine
We spin a web of magic
    affirming
  sacred sexuality**

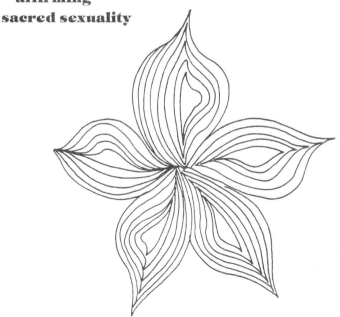

Maedel

I see you in a spotless
        white starched apron
        over your blue uniform
I hear you calling "Mary Lee"
You are my Black mother
        disguised as a maid

You gave me baths
You held me
You comforted me when I fell
You sang me your soul

        a white woman
I cannot know your struggles
        your pain
I can honor you and
    thank you for what
        you gave me

Now, I sing your soul to others
        sending your love
        to many that your life
        would never touch

Mother

I can learn to accept you
      as you are
I can accept the way you love me
      though
It isn't the way I want you to
I understand more clearly
What birthing and raising me
      cost you
As I birth and raise and
      let go of
      my own offspring

Mindy

Sometimes, if you feel I don't value you,
    my daughter,
    what I am feeling is
    how hard it is to value
    myself and where I've been
I hurt when I see you
    being so like
        my younger self
It's hard to forgive myself for
    past mistakes
    when I see them hurting you

I want to separate your present
    from my past
I ask you to separate your future
    from my present
Separation brings forgiveness and respect

We are alike but we are not
    each other

Georgia

I miss you
 now that you're gone
I'm proud that you
 take care of yourself
 —all on your own—
I'd like to take care of you
 and
 know that you need
 to do it yourself

I can learn to let go

my sister

You teach English in a community college
   in the South
You give excellent critique
   of my poetry
You have been thought illiterate
   by Northerners
   hearing your Southern accent
You ran for County Commissioner
   in a small Southern town
   and won
In 1982, you are the first woman ever
   to be an elected official in that county

I respect your choices
There are many ways to be a strong woman

What can I learn from Shirley?

I can learn to write precise
concise prose

What do I want from my friends?

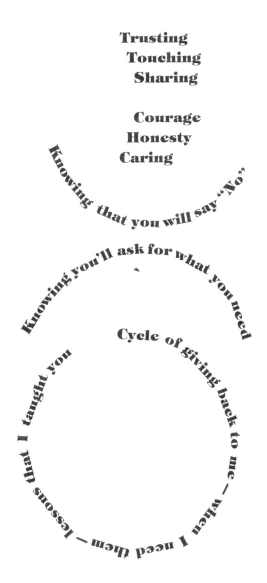

Trusting
Touching
Sharing

Courage
Honesty
Caring

Knowing that you will say "No"

Knowing you'll ask for what you need

Cycle of giving back to me — when I need them — lessons that I taught you

VII

What can I learn from learning?

What can I learn being first?

When I'm first, someone else
     is second
When someone else is first
     I'm second
Comparison leads to winners
     and losers
I don't want to be first   second
     or third
I want to be who I am
     valued for my unique self

There is no one like me

Superiority
implies
Inferiority

Long live difference

When I spoke and wrote at length
I was struggling to hear myself
The world was drowning me out
    with "Don't . . .
        "You can't . . .
        "Thou shalt not . . .

I took me many years of talk
    to be able to speak the language
      of poetry
     and know myself
    sensing affirming centered

What can I learn from learning?

I can learn that
 there's always more
 to know
I can learn to know
 and grow and change
 as long as
 I'm alive